Damnation
and
Cotton Candy

To Quintin,
Best Regards,
Alan

Damnation and Cotton Candy

Poems best served with hot cocoa, melancholy, and a sharp knife

Alan S. Kessler

Softcover ISBN: 978-1-938394-79-9

Ebook ISBN: 978-1-938394-80-5

Library of Congress Control Number: 2022910498

Cover art: Alan S. Kessler

Cover design and layout: Grace Peirce

published by
Leviathan Books

Contents

Good Business

A mother sifted flour for her son's birthday cake;
now in eternal commemoration of him
the desert sieves through his blanched rib bones
sand bleached of blood by the sun.
There are other bones near him, ancient ones,
baking on small shields and short swords—
Lust Fighters wanting land, trinkets, the joy of battle!
But he grew into his uniform by eating Sacred Ideals.

At a banquet table rats were too proud to join,
Politicians and Generals ate kidneys and loins, some of it animal,
(hard to tell where the suet ended and the men's hands began)
Black tailcoat pockets stuffed with bribes,
cascading medals bounced on Generals' tummies,
always room for an industrialist at the feast—
if he brought the mustard gas.
Flags! Anthem! Shrieking metal thunder!

"God punish the enemy!"
"Pass the money!"

Little boy in his big boy uniform too small to cover his bones.
Gone is the sound of the drum,
his last thought the blue icing on his birthday cake.

Oh Poseidon!

We comfort knowing
the silent seas of you
where entrails
of levers and lights
launch life's protectors
to incinerate the world.

Oh Poseidon!

Protector us
children of the great Admiral
who made a god out of nothing
but a dream of war,
a vision,
praise him too!
When thinking caused us pain
he saw them lurking,
he and the other smart ones
gave us to you

Oh Poseidon!

How wonderful your stomach,
how sweet your bowels,
they hold so much!
Rats eat our cities
the hungry cry
Of course!
So great a god *must* devour everything!

Open your silos
seed the skies
spear us as fish
we joyful squirm on your Trident
pierced so we can live—

Oh Poseidon!

Waiting

Through stunted trees along a forgotten road
a floating pale ray from the cloud covered moon
lights clusters of white moths on brittle black branches,
the desiccated bodies shrouded in tatters of web.

Silent and thin the moths drift in the wind,
return without memory, without regret,
from this insentient flight as the light floats on
to the road's end.

Here—

Cast by the moon's last fading breath
the shadow of a gate almost touches, before disappearing,
a broken headstone as nameless but less imposing
than the small crumbling rocks holding it up.

Brambles above him,
the gray meshed twists of thorns and briars press down,
dark are the bower vines wrapping his eyes, binding his tongue,
in this trackless wasteland of unhaunted sameness and memory.

He always remembers.
How terrible the curse.

Thumbs in suspenders, straw hat to the side, he merrily rocked
their picnic boat. They kissed. They loved. A promise to wed—

His words eaten in trenches
by bloated rats devouring bloated bodies,
by generals in chalets dipping their fat fingers in caviar
and toasting the next offense in goblets of wine mixed with blood.

He returned, not to her, but to belladonna's unfurling black cape.
The drinking.
The lost life.
The forgotten grave.

He remembers her eyes

     Mullen stew and potato pie

Catching white butterflies fluttering toward the sky…

A curse? No.
What is life but memories?
The only death, to be forgotten.

Here—

"I think this is it."

A young woman wearing jeans and a Grateful Dead T-shirt
foils the stone, gently touches the name she sponged back from time.

And the gate swings closed.

Why Politicians Send Others to War

To become the casualties these leaders need when writing autobiographies of contrition about their geopolitical mistakes.

My Prayer

Form my hand earth forge of the fire sun,
hammer, wind, my chest into rings of steel,
for I am dirt and factory, the planter of seed,
the maker of this small world and I belong to you.

On heaving, blood soaked shore I hear the carnival:
fat jolly clown wheezing to make people laugh,
pieces of his voice inside fragmentation mines;
bells, whistles, the explosions.
It's hot today, lemonade hot,
I smell popcorn and cotton candy, know in Centerville
families after church, honking like geese, go to the rides.
My son is there.
His little hand reaches out lost.
I lie with others in this hole of skin,
watch with eyes melted open a red balloon float across
the blue white sky.
I love carnival day.
The ground sings, my guts move, drip, ooze,
I lie as still as warm taffy—
but you know that.

I have climbed in lightning charged rain
to connect wires so a hospital can see,
I have taken my bright police badge into dark hallways
where silence waits for me—

I am a single mom with a young son who never smiles—

I have done all you ask.

Form my being from thunder, make me steel and rock
even if it's to silently endure those who live by eating me
and thinking my sweaty flesh sweet.

Grant me life, sacrifice, toil, love and pain,
through your grace never let me become a parasite
or forsake you by genuflecting to those who take
the surplus profit of workers to build estates over graves.

God of fire
God of the wind

    Amen

Southeast Downtown

To stride across a bleeding heart, sacred symbol on marble floors,
into cloistered mahogany rooms where supplicants wait
to serve on silver plates foreclosures
and blinded songbirds boiled alive in brandy,
no shame for these men and women
who with uncovered heads eat whole the debtors and birds
savoring the bones, for to them, God's anointed,
engorged by drilling and burning, it is written:

They shall have dominion
and digest the earth like worms
but give nothing back

Not worms but priests filling their table with pork and wine,
let the privileged come and partake while remembering
the gospel of wealth requires charity—eat gold flaked cake
but send a crispy wafer to the bum slipping on the wet grass
of his urinal under the overpass.

Blessed the charity of the saved who worship in Gothic Cathedrals
of steel and glass rising from ground hallowed by theft,
proud buildings infinitely replicating their soaring enormity
in the reflection from each other's windows,
a fast spreading city of plenty for the paper hands inside
who cross marble floors mopped by the small and unseen
and wearing pointed masks filled with viper flesh powder
can't smell in their courtyards, the centers of commerce,
the plague of addiction and poverty they caused by selling little pills.

Snakes with priestly heads and bodies of leveraged followers
all interconnected slither to helipads where they ascend toward Aspen—

Until the bodies lying unclaimed beneath riveted metal beams
hear the trumpets blow then rising with clenched fists
kneel before Christ down from his gimcrack plastic cross,
the Bansky shopping bags in his outstretched crucified palms gone,
the domes crumbling as their foundations of silver melt
      in a whirlwind of fire.

Insanity

One big tooth bites over a puffy lip,
droopy eyelids sadden blue eyes already dim.
Fed thawed chicken on paper plates by those returning home
to monogrammed china and warm bread,
sinews of the stringy meat toughened
the long tangles of his mud caked hair
gravel turned his coarse beard grey
while winter winds twisted it into knots.

His concrete beds warmed by defecating dogs and car exhaust
he slept under blankets of carbon monoxide laced with frost.
Underneath his coat of bright pink plastic fur
a wool topcoat donated by a man of business after his wife
found a loose thread in the cashmere of her filler-injected life.
Four different colored socks, sandals, pajama bottoms,
his face gouged by loss and ice.

Mothers hold their children close.
Others don't see him.
He shuffles mumbling

His hand holding smoke tastes the sweetness of leaves burning in snow
summer rain pouring drops of sand caresses his cheek
thunders the sound of mockingbird wings
silent, the noise of the city sings.
In an alley he watches the bar's neon bloom on frozen slime
everywhere there is light and time
memory and swings moving without rust
alive again beyond the alcohol beyond the dust
almost within reach a young girl's touch.

He doesn't carry an ax but mumbles stories
tan faces with silky teeth are too sane to hear
they'd rather mould the world into plastic
and on vacation sensibly drink champagne instead of water
while admiring between bites of shrimp the adorable children
digesting the phosphorus and lead served by computers
recycled in famine lands.

"The water's rising. Another martini, please."
Bland moon faces don't mumble they shout.
The tide is theirs—sexy and high
a frothy paradise of godliness
lasting forever until their fairylands die.

A Day at the Beach

Saw tooth sea
edges of waves salt stiffened
into mouths
dry and cracked
reaching to rake moisture
from the seeping sun.

Blistered spray
hissing against pitted rocks
stretching from husk water
to claw gray and parched
into black sand.

Hollow bellows the sound
below the ocean's crisp skin
a feverish curled membrane frying fish
while overhead crazed seagulls
try disgorging pieces of molten shell.

Alone on the beach
no one knows what I see
as I fill my cup with sunlight
and watch the ocean's acid move in
drop by drop

Not Me

Drop by drop the sun rains swirling mad gasses with skins of acid;
drop by drop, tinder and heat, now shimmering as if alive, the rain
    splatters,
sizzles, inside the fury of a convulsing wind too scorched to speak.

Descending into land heated and cracked into the shape of open mouths
gargling fire, the rain grows fields of ash,
rising, rising, on crematorium earth to ask:

"Where is the cooling blood?"

None in Terry, mummified by years relaxing in a beach chair,
she had stored her intestines and bronzed full stomach in canopic
    shopping bags.

No blood in Harold either. Afraid sharks might swim through his
    dining room window,
he built ever higher ocean homes. Never forgot to compost for his
    hanging gardens or
recycle his vodka bottles.

Bloodless too were the users of plastic forks and microwaves.

Ashamed God saw their nakedness, skeletons put on skin and ran
through the burning rain.

The only ones saved, those who had driven their electric cars to the safe
parts of Hell.

A Remainder of Touch

Patchwork fields of luminescent green only children hatched in moonlight
across the River Shannon can fully see, crackle with static electricity,
glossy obsidian flowers in sparking acidic grass reflect from blasted earth
to yellow sky the gray rainbow trails of stone-eyed butterflies.

Metal blossoms ring tin bells, dance in the smell of honey bramble
        and iodine pine,
centipede sequence of tiny winds fills sunshine with concrete
        and rubber pebbles,
fuses gently into a storm of mute thunder raining down lustrous organic
        beads exploding on the ground.

Reversing its flow to the thinning sea, fast flows the mercury stream
cutting a polished shine through the flowing sweep of fossilized
        meadowland,
a snake body full of energy rapidly cooling, exposing in its shrinking
        belly
delicate purple crystals pulsating over parsley and tongues turning to ice.

An Irish lad of webbed feet crawls from his shell onto the sand where
        poets once sang.
He is Poet now, birth to sunset his time to give what he feels unspoken
        sound.
Darkness gathers his broken pieces, children in the spawning patch
        listening.

Another, drenched in sulfur, rises to become the next voice of souls,
he too disappearing into this place of velvety moonlight falling into
moaning, jagged glass.

All Life is Connected

Thin silver serpent coiling twin heads with ruby eyes
Hisses silently from glass tongues coated in diamond sparkles,
Its black marble rattler, topped by a drop of gold, twitches imperceptibly.
Rainforest jewelry of the Company's daughter who wears such pieces
On more appropriate occasions.

Silent passage through leaf and vine humid and sticky,
among blackened stumps, in pools of fleshy roots,
over bones and nests, the smell of hunted flesh,
feeling warmth, only this, from hearts swallowed beating—

To stop and not move, the water reverberating,
metal and men raking across the land.

    The snake lifts its head.

The Company's daughter nods with hers while acknowledging the toasts
At this fund raiser for her charity, Friends of Apes.
A few smiles, not too many, the real party is waiting.
Outside, she reaches into her bag for her serpent necklace,
Doesn't see the waiting eyes, glowing and red.

Simple Faith

God exists and made Hell justice
for a man who on a summer day
took a little girl and left behind
her pink bike, wheel spinning.

I believe in Heaven too.

Another View

Nestled snuggly in an ammonia and methane blanket,
suckled on sugar and phosphate, RNA grows cellular wide hips,
female eyes twinkle at male ones engorged with DNA
and on the hunt.

High energy for a bit of pleasure sequenced in to continue life...

    Reproduce.

    Die.

Fill up the white spaces inside.

    With all the thrashing,
    with all the lust,
    comes glorious creation,
    the new gods of dust.

Predestination

The dim light from mourners' candles fogs cold
giving crystalline breath to gargoyles, serpents, and winged demons,
empty torch holders along a black marble wall covered in spiny ice.
Burning low, the candles' pale glow rests on neatly stacked bones,
shudders out into darkness as if never there,
into silence except for a rat sliding across the floor's smooth snow.

How peacefully they remember their prayers spoken for a girl
still flesh and raven hair, eyes closed in sleep, only this, it seemed.
Certain of salvation, their pew well worn, they sip hot spiced wine
with Elder Smith who wiggles his toes by the fire.

Chants gone, the air cleansed of incense by decay,
the wind seeps in rocking her body. Her candles stone,
their fire shards of ice, she mourns the living,
shrouding themselves in myth,
unwilling to enjoy the sweetness of dying summer
by seasoning their winter days with acceptance of oblivion.

Down from the wall the stacked bones fall, her frozen eye splits open,
draining a tear onto the wisps of her remaining white hair
her head resting on a stained silk pillow.

Here

A dog sniffs leaves, chases its tail, plays with other dogs, dies.
How nice...for a dog.

I want the book,
any book will do
if its symbols promise immortality.

I will follow my leader into the jungle,
cover myself with a dark cloth and wear new sneakers,
die waiting for a space ship.
I've always enjoyed traveling.

A 6000 year old fruit tree!
Burn the skin into mine
then dance around me
while I stand naked
and eat its olives.

All I want is to live forever.

Except...what is that?

Eternal thoughts, cerebral contemplation of the cosmic order?
Endless perfecting? Loss of me? Loss of others?
Unending longing for football and ice cream?

Maybe dogs have the answer.

The Eulogy I Wish I'd Given

How many words have been spoken over the dead?
Enough to create another atmosphere,
one of sadness and lost dreams
extending far into space,
into a nothingness where even cold
has no meaning.

When someone dies at 45
When the good husband, good father, good brother, friend,
have all been said and we are left after the crematorium door closes
with a life turned into ashes,

Why didn't God intervene?
Why does He save some while letting the hearts of others explode?
Does He have a sense of humor, thinks fat jokes are funny,
or are there divine rules, a cosmic order only the insane understand?

Maybe He's indifferent.

Maybe He's not there.

Except...

On the day my brother-in-law died alone, in his bedroom, in the
        afternoon,
his two young children visited a friend down the street instead
of going home after school and rushing upstairs to hug dad.

A miracle, given by a comedic god in one of his lucid moments.

Talisman

Tightrope over a windy gorge
"Be careful!" The girlfriend's words
spiraling hollow toward the river below
even before she turns and smiles
at the TV reporters;
stacked blonde hair and tall white boots
accent pieces for her shiny miniskirt
she shifts pink glistening skin into the camera's angle
while her boyfriend totters overhead.

"Be Careful"
Really?
Did he need a reminder?
At least she was honest,
knew her words were meaningless except for show.

"Have a safe trip," without which I'd turn my car
into the path of a truck.
"Take care."
I think I packed it with my socks and underwear.
"Good night. "Pleasant Dreams."
Thank you. I promise not to have any nightmares.

"My condolences."
How nice. I feel better already.

Life denied order,
the organizing forces of nature only for particles,
we weave our tightropes from magical words
hoping they span the chaos
Good luck the only incantation
that doesn't make an asteroid laugh
as it waits for its chance to smile at the cameras.

Winter Night

Pine boards old over ginger,
the cloudy apple color
of Indian Summer cider rows.
Cracker barrel hoops in oxblood metal,
on sawdust,
a passing twist of calico,
honey centered rolls.
Oil lamps warming windows,
coating glass against the wind
while cinders from Franklin's potbelly
reddens rock candy in canisters of tin

Emptied dark veins, the branches fall black
against snow, the sky unforgiving.
Scratched deep by ice after each December storm,
the tree's frozen stigmata shows a man lost in the wind.
No one remembers him or why they call
this store of crackers and warm candy,
                            "Jeb's"

Winter Night Bay

Silver tone trees in crystalline mist
crowed together like rumpled balls
of metallic paper set on sticks of dark ice.

Swirling ocean wind suspending in passage
concentric patterns of frozen emerald brine
released to lash the fresh water storm
lashing the land with waves of pebble hail.

Wind chime willows bending in lonely sound
into winter, into night, but leaving for last touch
clouds folded over to reflect as pink coals do
the emerging twilight sun.

Image feelings of another time
shattered now by remembering.

Monkey World

"Metaphors are organic, Sweetie."

She flicks a few ashes into her potted petunia.

"Let's see…he was—like piss hitting a doublewide's roof! Perfect!
Sums up the man: his coarseness, shallowness, trailer park mentality.
Piss, piss, piss," the word dribbling off her lips.

Actually my dad was shit and we lived in a large Tudor.
But she's Alpha so I hunch down, give her a banana, and take my story
of a successful businessman turned serial killer back for another rewrite.
I have an advance. She keeps me watered and fed.

No one is more important than Boss Man.

He farts expansively in his tailored Armani suit, scratches his nuts,
-urinates on my shoe, shows me his erect penis.

He's old. I'm waiting. After we hunt him, fillet him,
give each board member a piece, I'll be Boss Man smoking his cigars.
Everyone will watch me, of course.
Let them.

I'll wear his skin.

Everyone Loves Cookies

I am cookie man

so soft and round

a doughy shape made fresh daily

anyway you slice me or pound

I'm not a fat roll or an ugly muffin

and misshaped cookies burn in the oven

Perfect dough you can't earn or win

births perfect cookies for cookie tins—

I'm one of them! Tiny nuts and powdered sugar skin!

"Will you march holding a sign?"

Give me the words and I'll be right in line

"The votes are counted, the blind child dies."

Of course. Everyone else has bright raisin eyes.

I am cookie press me press me

I am cookie press me man!

"Really? You seem so somber

terribly dark and cobweb spun."

That's just my face, I'll change it,

24

take a bite, I'm lots of fun!

"Very good. Now swallow your tongue."

(A guttural *Heil* followed by a big, butter pecan smile)

Death Penalty

Where the moon shines black
in an alleyway paved by gravestones
my father comes to answer.

He is a soldier.

"Want to see the sword I took from a dead Jap?"

No. Isn't there something else? My baby book?

His smirk slaps my face.

He is an accountant.

"Made lots of money from tax shelters. Horses, phony corporations,
    orange groves,
the rich always look for ways to screw the IRS. Sure, the penalties and
    interest
cost them but that was years later. What did they expect? Nothing lasts,
not even me."

What about mother?

"Great times! Flew the Concorde to Paris, owned a restaurant and
    nightclub,
don't remember all the women I had. Did everything I wanted for as
long as I could."

Mother?

"You were always weak."

What if I kill too? Will you love me?

Dismissing me with a fart, he disappears, leaving behind the taste
of my insignificance. *But maybe, on a summer day, we can play catch...*

He is a murderer.

Hear the murmuring of the family he killed by shooting a young man?
His daughter stares into a mirror, hoping her best friend will again smile
    back;
his wife wrinkles inside.

I am obscene. My questions insult the dead. How terrible to want love
from this creator of death who changed a family into a bullet hole.

My father didn't come to answer.

My father is blood.

The Unveiling

Not a gravestone
just a plaque
in green grass
near a rubber band airplane
a child lost when visiting
someone else.

His name.
WWII veteran.
Purple Heart.
Date of birth. Date of death.
Beloved something,
the plaque just big enough
for this incompleteness.

Cloudless afternoon, mid-June,
no shade over the grave.
I stand dutifully sweating.
His skin easily tanned,
bronze, like the marker
we should have buried.

I do grieve. Not for him.
The others do. I understand.
He loved them.
In pretend flight
I hold the airplane high
and play among the dead.

Uncle Joe

When peritonitis should have killed father,
saved him from tearing the sky,
Uncle Joe took us for a ride on a summer night
so we wouldn't worry—
crazy mother, a sister, and me,
bouncing in his old jeep.
Fat, suspender wearing Uncle Joe
who was never a dad but showed me how to whittle
and gave me all his little pocket knives.

Hospital over,
he probably screwed a nurse or two,
father proudly showed us his ruptured appendix
stored in a mason jar. He liked trophies.

Uncle Joe died with a piece of herring in his mouth,
father chewed his steak well;
in his gold Cadillac,
wearing silk suits and Countess Mara ties,
he gave rides to his girlfriends so he needn't worry
about what they had seen.

Father's Day

Deep raspberry color staining violent across
goose-fleshed asphalt, the cinnabar of a death mark
all that's left of the old car he bought
after exchanging his gold nugget necklace and leisure suit
for the plot that would dress him in Death Row diapers.

Drifting across an old stone wall, amber light sways gently
on the spider's lacework where a white feather hangs between
beads of dew; petals dry in the center of a broken clay pot.
Father splashed it all with beer,
squashed the spider in his hand.

Seen against starlight, each rising bubble of croaking
and cricket song break at dawn,
a worm family dancing to the music.
Father had heavy boots.
He picked up the rest for fishing.

I didn't know what the word meant.
Father didn't care about anything I said,
but I guess it gave him a reason
to push me down the stairs.

On dirty asphalt where his shitty car disintegrated
because he could no longer afford even rust,
there's just some faded crud and me standing, remembering him.

Happy Father's Day.

Gram

It's been 17 years since she died,
17 years.

My sister saw light on a mirror,
a kiss good-bye, she said.
But Gram loved me, rubbed my legs when they ached,
hated The Snake forever, the name she gave a 5 year old
for pushing me once in a game.

Not that I expected a Raven on the bust of Pallas
or planks creaking down my long hallway at midnight,
a whisper
a tap
a penny found on its edge
or strand of gray hair floating in lamplight
would have been enough for me,
one small wonder for a true believer in ghosts.

But my sister knows
when the dead say good-bye
they place a single silver tear on glass,
in the night,
for those they thought cared.

(I didn't call her, she was dying.
I loved her too much for that)

26 years without Gram now,
26 years.

Room Down the Hall

They closed her door
talk in whispers
but I don't know why.

It's time for my
True Life detective story
read by gray eyes using different voices,
filled with lungs of smoke
from the cigarettes she rolls in Bugle Boy paper,
big smiles, floppy teeth,
she hits me too but I never feel it.

True Life detective time
on a mother-away day—
except today she isn't away
visiting her head doctor
but at home whispering with the door closed.

I put on shadows and at the door
secretly push it open.
The smoke is gone and the denture smiles.
In the thick, hard to breath dark,
I see her sleeping too neatly,
no crumbs, no bloody magazines.

I sneak in and stretch out beside her.
I have stories.
I can whisper too.

Grandfather's Place

A wrinkled finger materializing on a broken mirror
beckons me down the hall in a house of brittle racing sheets
and empty bottles.

Inside the small room of a dust covered, one-eyed stuffed bear,
through the silent thinness of scattered haze,
his shadow crosses a child's overturned chair.

I stop to whisper.
Grandfather, I am here.

Pipe smoke rises in a phosphorous cloud
illuminating flaring, wild whitehair and blue eyes that look at me sadly.

"Buried beneath the willow out back is a jar of pennies,
marbles in an old cigar box, two tin airplanes, and my junior G Man
    badge.
There's something else, tied in a string. Dreams."

My suit and tie speak.
Grandfather, you're dead.

Yellowed paper, bottles on the floor,
I am alone in the night, nothing more.

Reality

Silver pocket watch touched smooth into warm metal,
open its case to the fading sound of its old worn chimes
as he put his hand over mine and we rode in a black carriage
down cobble streets, past shop and pub,
the gas lamps' light making small holes in the covering dark.

Click, click, tick, hands across the face of an eagle,
deeper still into the spin and whirl of tiny levers and wheels
inside it, inside my mind,
with the power to stop time.

His skin is here, his voice too on our merry rides;
traces of smoke from his briar pipe, or was it clay or wood?

A little shop on a back street, its few cobblestones
the only ones in a city without night.
I hold the watch.
I've made it grandfather's.
I didn't know him, now I do.

He loves me.
That's better than memory.

* Mother

* Some poems don't require words

Nowy Swiat (New World)

My parents were as country as Jeffrey Dahlmer was a sous-chef
still they named my sister *Debbie Sue.*

After Stalin used German soldiers and Polish blood as site preparation
for a new Warsaw of concrete blocks becoming grayer with each
        industrial rain,
the Soviet Union built in the city, as a gift to the Polish people,

The Palace of Culture

which was neither a palace nor cultural but looked in its high and spreading
overbearing mass as if the Empire Sate Building had mated with a tumor.

On street Nowy Swiat, Magda wore a brown, goat fur goat she'd shortened,
a hat made from her father's, boots—
green eyed, well styled Magda standing beautiful on hard snow
after a meeting of her lots-of-cigarettes lots-of-talk movie club.

The bus was late.

Prowling in one of the few cars in Warsaw, old but young looking Marion
using hunter skills convinced Magda to come in from the cold.

She followed him to Miami,
Married. Divorced.

At a party, red borsch spilled on the pants of a white suit. Magda was there.
She knew how to save clothes.

We married. Satish hired her.
We introduced him to my sister,
Debbie Sue

A sudden cardiac arrest.

She wears a funeral sari as Satish crackles among lotus flowers
and his rice cakes float to the sea.

New World, Debbie Sue, because the bus was late on Nowy Swiat.

Wings

Wings:

Dark wind heavy in the heat of August,
beats the night into tatters,
stretches across the bones of dead branches
the flapping skin of darkness
impenetrable and mad with fever.

Wings:

Broken shutters, broken doors,
coffin lids banging in abandoned rooms
above tumbling stairs,
in forgotten places buried by thick summer air,
where words evaporate as we speak.

Still, some remember:

clear streams
fishing cane pole and bobber
ice cream melting faster than our tongues could eat
baseball in a lot
the feel of light
the smell of weeds and grass
friends...

Now dead...

Gray scarred arms heavy with membranes of fat
try lifting our bodies to the height of kites,
to the moon we stand and cast out our hands,
Where are the haunted places of summer?
Will you help us fly?

Burns the asphalt at our feet,
on us summer skeletons cling,
this the answer of Wings.

Looking Glass

Its faded iodine tinged name
blending in among bluebells
and whorls of purple sage,
an old milk carton with dirt in its belly
tilts in the shade near broken glass,
the long scrape
down the waxen side
a child marking the instant
his daydreaming in a woodland field
turned summer clouds into dragons.

What can bring him back?

Blow hard now,
hard into a red carnival balloon
pressed into the carton's chambers
Blow until the bright ball explodes
sending balloon skin
and wax fragments back into time...

Only to fall
as all broken balloons and old milk cartons do,
into an old man's vacant eyes
and on shards mirroring ill-formed clouds
he will never again see streak the sky
with dragon fire.

Norwoods

Whispers of the brittle wind trapped inside silence. The dried fibrous rain of leaves on old thick shoes block shaped as if hacked from the ground. Along a weed tangled path, man-feet muted by the past cross into this place of darkness where hanging shadows hoping for a sliver of moonlight twist overhead.

Now a strange creature grown beyond all proportion rightful for swings in summer or sandcastles at the sea, I stop to listen. From beneath tattered flags, at a dust covered table set with cracked goblets and broken plates, its center piece a pirate chest of bones, does he call me across time?

Clod feet heavy on frozen ground, I have found in this forgotten lot the ruins of a carnival ...

They were—
Cotton candy days, caramel apple stacking,
popcorn crackle popping days of shiny whiz bang
scoop machines and slithering things that hid in
dark creepy corners of Professor Barnaby's Mausoleum
of Ancient Mummified Remains, waiting, patiently,
for little children to eat.

For only a dime, thrills inside space ships exploring
planets on wings, spinning in screams, while on the ground
little sisters and brothers, holding melting ice cream
and balloons on strings, wore *gen-u-wine,* imported,
one-of-a-kind plastic carnival rings.

On the puffing white smoke clink clank train
of animal cars with brightly covered seats carrying
happy jumping feet, fathers with cameras and mothers in hats,
sat a few seats back from boys and girls who couldn't sit down
as the train passed miniature bridges and cardboard towns.
I loved the sound of the woo woo whistle in summer air--

If I listen closely it's almost still here.

Flashing lights, bright green orange clashing lights,
pinned to wheels that buckled us in for fast whirling spins,

capturing our breath in merging circles of hot neon haze,
in flickering image frames from old movie days, we white knuckled
gripped the restraining strip and shouted our fright,
twirled by the night, like taffy!

Pipe steaming, cymbal banging, Kaleidoscope calliope,
music synchronized to the up down, forward circling round
of the carrousel's hand painted horses who with happy fixed faces
and outflowing manes raced proudly while I pulled the reins.

"Faster, Duster!" my words lost in the rush of wind across
their blue glass eyes.

"Come on, three balls to hit me in, just one on the bull's-eye,
and I lose, you win!" the little man with the high pointed cap,
shaggy, baggy, puff ball suit, hard sounding laugh, called to us
as we stood in front of the Dump the Clown booth in the game section
one-half of the Norwoods Amusement park.

A tall, skinny man holding his girlfriend's hand
pushed past my friend and me and said he'd be happy to see
if he could dump the clown in.

"Hope Bozo can swim!" the man added with a grin.

He paid his money, took off his leather jacket, aimed at the target,
but didn't whack it, the ball flying by, fast and high.

"My, my, not a very good throw, not much to show your gal!"
the clown shouted. "If you want my advice, free just for today,
better let her have the next play, she ain't gonna do no worse
than you, *he he he*," the clown grinning big and mean
as the second ball harmlessly hit the screen.

The clown rattled his chair, told the girl she had real pretty hair.
"Why someone like you should go out with me--" then *eeeeeeeeeeee*
to the sound of gongs and bells, the clown fell into very cold looking
      water.

      Brrrrr I said to my friend who rubbed his arms and shivered,
      also pretending.

Proud his third toss had rung the bell, the man bowed for
the clapping, cheering crowd, but the clown sput sput sputtered
to the top, shook himself free, and with one upward hop, shot out
of the water and over the side to neatly slide in a flopping shoe glide,
to his carnival chair suspended once more in the air.

The clown sat down. Then leering, jeering, in anger half-rearing,
again began taunting and making a racket, all directed
toward the man in the black jacket.

"A mighty lucky fling that doesn't mean a thing
'cause you'll never again knock me in! Want to try?
It'll cost you another two bits, what you make in tips
for walking ladies' poodles!"

The man flushed red, angrily shook his oil slick head,
then pounded his quarter right down while squinting in hate
at the clown, who was, by then, merrily dancing a jig, bulging
his eyes, tipping his wig.

Away we skipped, but I stopped to see the man slam his fist
against the base of a tree after another ball he threw missed its mark.
Faster than his jibber, jibber, jabber, I outran the clown's
laughter, trying to follow me.

Plink, plink, pop, popping gun shots at marching bears
and birds in the air, at trap door up-springing tigers on trees,
snarling through plastic leaves, before disappearing again with a
snapping clink into the metal ground.

Spoke circles of orange black wedges whose very edges
were numbered or lettered, spun around in click click sound as
eyes watched waiting to win. Striped shirted men wearing red
arm bands and against the glare, green visors pulled low over
curly black hair, scooped up the dimes and yelled,
    "*We have a WINNA over here!*"
as they handed stuffed giraffes or pink and black pandas
to teens in bandannas whose faces, twisted by sneers,
looked like they'd found them in the House of Mirrors.

Red slurpy syrup poured over ice, waffle sandwiches

gooshing ice cream out the sides, heaped cardboard plates
of vinegary French fries, slices of "Mother McCreary's Home
Made Hot Apple Pie" taffy, caramels, and chunks of rock candy,
wasn't it just dandy eating yourself sick between rides!

"Come on, let me put your name on one,"
the bald man with a long string tie called to me as we walked by
his booth of hats.

And the kinds he had!

Round with multi-colored feathers, tall made out of authentic
almost leather, cowboy hats and pirate caps and in spaceman helmets
inter-galactic radio flaps for over the ears!

I reached in my pocket, found only a dime, Tommy added
fifteen cents to mine—not enough, well some other time...

We bought one brightly colored balloon! With a big smiling face
of the Man-in-the-Moon! Zzzzzzzzzzt from the silver, gas blower-
upper machine, a quick blur of fingers tying the string, and it was ours!

I took the balloon and let it drift above my head,
it tugged followed me wherever I led, but someplace between
the steel dart throw and the only in town nickel Skee-Ball roll,
the balloon floated away into the night, winking at me as it
bob bob bobbed out of sight.

Heart shaped necklaces and jingle jangle chains,
crosses and stars arranged in lanes on pieces of black velvet,
rings with staring lion faces, rings with shiny stones set in carved places,
bracelets and pins and earrings piled in tins, then to engrave it all,
at the back of the stall behind a torn screen, the sparking, whirling,
Electro Dynamic Metal Etching Machine waiting for Tommy and me
to get close!

Ha! What a joke!

It never made us ghosts...

When the lights of the Norwoods Amusement park flashed twice, rides stopped and men began covering the booths and games. We stayed until the park turned dark, then walked home happy knowing there would be other nights to twirl and scream and eat cotton candy.

And there were.

For a few summers more.

Heavy footsteps through an empty lot. Where a clown once slid back on his chair, his grin bright, I stand in darkness. The train is gone, taking with it the children. Where do lost balloons go?

A sound! Louder as I hurry toward it …Only this…the Norwoods Amusement Park sign banging against a post, the words faded and cracked. I touch my face. A dangling, forgotten rope twists its shadow in the night.

It's late. I should hurry. The dinner is for me, Man of the Hour, the soon-to-be recipient of a crystal vase. I have a low handicap and understand the market. My wife is in Palm Beach. My mistress never tells me I'm fat. Ahead is the gate leading outside if only I can touch its iron spikes.

I look back. I did hear him. At the table near Barnaby's Mausoleum, Tommy stands, smiles, offers me his hand.

The Head
(For the kiddies)

New here, huh doc? Want to hear my story?

It was a head, almost human from a distance 'cept of course that the
head was wormwood with hinges at the mouth and although the eyes
looked like they was the thinking kind that didn't seem natural for ones
made of glass.

Me and Pete had paid to see the Alligator Man and finding out we'd
    been gypped,
he was just some guy in a bowling shirt, rubber snout and tail,
we decided to sneak
into all the other shows but got caught the first time we tried
by a man in a checkered vest,
his nose as big as a sausage. I would have used my hunting knife
but Pete kicked him in the shin and we ran—

Straight into the tent of the head. There it was, on top a box. No one
else around, real dark too, and the smell the same as Grammy's, greasy
    and sweet.
They found her just the way I left her, dead in a chair. Don't be sad,
    they said.
Her smell stayed on me until I sliced up the clothes I had worn and
buried them and her crochet pillow in the backyard.

Again, that old Grammy sweat trying to kill me. Pete didn't help.

I hated the way he breathed—little bubbling wheezes only someone
with good ears like mine could hear.
In that tent, his breath on my neck,
he added other sounds on purpose. *I know he did.*
A rattle. A snort. Clicking in his nose. I wanted to cut it off.

We walked closer to the head.

I saw it was falling apart: an eyeball bulged, rotted wood showed
    underneath
cracks wrinkling the painted green skin, not real green, more like the

44

color lamplight
gives snakes at night when they make the mistake of sliding into an
    outhouse I'm using.
Suddenly those blue glass eyes looking at me turned as white as slugs in
    moonlight,
boney arms shot out of the box rolling toward us.

"I need a new head," the hinge-jaw flapped. "Can I have yours?"

Never met a squirrel or cat I couldn't gut quickly. Pete must have been
    impressed.
He quit trying to annoy me with his breathing. It stopped, just like
    that.

You can loosen the straps.
I've got weak boney arms and blind white eyes.
All the doctors here know I'm harmless.

Another Poem For The Little Ones
(Best read at bedtime)

Perhaps you have seen in the shadows of night
Spectral faces of supernatural might
Ghostly forms with deep rich sighs
Drifting with fangs across the bloody moon sky

Perhaps you have heard that moss covered moan
Subterranean calling from a graveyard home
The eerie cry of a withered head
Asking you to join it in the land of the dead

Maybe you've watched your closet door creak open
And a skeleton rattle out with eyes fiery and molten
Who with snapping jaw and acid drool
Shuffles closer to chop a kiss down on you

Dear child I'm here to say this is nothing but bunk
There are no crawling hands inside your trunk
No spiders or snakes, no withered heads,
Nothing hiding in your closet or under your bed

There is one small thing, really too silly to mention
In a dark forest in its darkest deadest section
Poisoned seed grew into a flesh eating tree
A child's bed made of that wood would be crazy, agreed?

When you're asleep would it bite your neck first or shred your knee?
Do you think your mom and dad would hear you scream?

Childhood Path

Where flying heroes thud down onto warrior sticks
and the trail of summer hotdog mustard ends
at a jumble of lost camp lanyards, grass stained baseballs,
forever, sworn in blood, best friends—

Here clubhouse doors open only in the wind,
distant but near, children jumping rope chant as if not dead—

> *where is mary*
> *where is she*
> *kick the can deary deary*
> *once for mary*
> *once for me*

Mary
and the little boy who wanted to fly.
How nicely they sit during boardroom meetings
about toilet bowl cleaners and denture cream,
never fidgeting, their flesh boiled in coffee,
eaten in pieces, especially tasty their brains.

"All it takes gentlemen and, um, Miss, is to exorcize dreams.
We aren't barbarians. You're still alive.

"Let's make a few missiles from the stars!"

> *he flew here*
> *he flew there*
> *he wore a cape*
> *and flew everywhere*

Dead children living in the remains of men and women
who remember and silently chant the rhymes
while sitting eyes closed at dinner tables so as not to see
their faces in the lacquered plates.

Ghost Child

The smell of gasoline.
Maybe someone is filling a generator in their yard
or a car at the station down the street,
could be a boat.
Gas makes spark-ignited engines run.
That's its purpose.
But what if it leaks?
How can randomness be the essence of anything?

My bottle of cream soda and the brine encrusted pickle
scooped from a barrel at what we called the Little Store,
a bite, a swig of pop, I can ride my bike no hands!

There's where Wilma Jones used to live, that brown house on Cassidy.
We were in second grade when she moved away three years ago.

Nan left this year, right before Thanksgiving.

We weren't friends but she was in my class.
Some of the guys were mean, they called her peg-leg
after the doctors cut her leg off to stop the cancer.
It didn't.
Mack told me she had died.
I remember not knowing what to feel.

I was sad when Wilma moved away but I knew she was alive—
someplace. What was Nan? Nothing?
When you're thirsty you drink pop,
when hungry a pickle is good but so is blue raspberry taffy.
A heart is supposed to keep beating. That's why we have one.
I don't understand.

I never ride my bike past Nan's old house.

A slicker flashes yellow through rain,
the child turns, distant eyes touching mine.
"Nan?"
I have never forgotten her, that's my emotion,

and like handlebars on a bike ridden with no hands,
maybe there is no purpose. We are, then we're not,
and the ghosts we conjure never speak.

Mayfly

For cool swagger in 3rd grade recess
sucked on butter rum hard candy
bought from old Bob at the Little Store
who moved as stiffly as the crank on his register
and used his milky white eye to keep us away
from dipping our hands into the pickled eggs.

I always had to wear white socks
even with an oversized black funeral suit
Uncle Joe dead.

Where is this boy,
the one who made a lopsided tie rack
for DAD, letters formed from nail holes?

In a purple Cadillac gunned down Broad Street,
red eyes in the center of long fins,
an 18 year old wanting to show *everyone*
there was no old fart inside.

With Mary
very plain
until she brushed her hair forward and back.

Along a twilight crimson beach,
a son held high, looking into his eyes,
turning, turning, into the night...

To stand alone.

There is an old fart inside
the morphine drip of passing time,
all anyone sees is what we are now
and even we forget the layers of our heart.

It

It, just an It, that's what she said
while walking away from me.

I remember It
I don't need to see an empty swing,
the supermarket's quarter ride will do,
all I can put on the horse's saddle
is my bag of tomatoes.

I ate my roommate's cold pizza
but would have found the money
to take care of It.
I told her.

I didn't get to.

Sometimes at night
in the drifting time before sleep
I'll tickle It lying weightless beside me.

He never laughs.

Dreams

Once when I was young
and in the quiet of dream
I saw the summer wind
hunt a lady.

From behind a palm
near sand covered stone
the wind waited, swirled high
to catch her wheat-colored hair
flung sassily at the sky,
hearing only laughter
as she ran by.

A moment ago
the wind didn't hide,
heavy with grizzled ice
it never left the old man's side,
wind and man formed a team,
and in sweat, I awoke, in the night,
remembering both dreams.

Returning Home

On dust path rise on a warm September morning,
a deep inhaling moment to taste red raspberries
at the hedgerow and glide my hand through the lily thick pond
where I had played with my toy boat, pond water an ocean,
lily pads the island hideouts of pirates.

Old fences also try keeping me in.
Don't they know? I'm 17!
Roll up cotton sleeves!
Hitch my pants high!
Jump the last gate!
A tip of the hat to Sunday awakening her face to church,
kind face, loving one,
but not mine.
The pathway down is between thick trees,
(this whole place is ancient)
my shoes are tight but new.
I hobble away in the early morning light.
(I'll write)

*

Heavy layers of snow wrapped by mid-winter around trunks
drop the rotted wood into the path I stumble along,
the fallen rocks around me skinned by ice.
It's dark. It's cold.
I pull my tattered coat together, wheeze a few steps uphill.
Ahead is her home, if only I could see it.
With shaking hand I light a match—
the wind blows it out.
No matter, I've found my little boat.
My cold breath its steam, we'll sail away.

An Old Tree

When my mind walked on winter roads or ice-blanketed fields of silence
When my thoughts centered inward in pain yet could explode outward
To consume the sky with fire
When the pathway's end promised it would start again beyond the next
    hill
I'd walk to this place where the rocks slide deep and offer for the
    willow's keep
the shadows of my heart.

With my hand on time, on the scarred over cuts of initials and rhymes,
Its green sap flowed through my veins and I became the cells of a tree
Full of sunlit wind and rain, of soft seasons and hard, all tasting alive.

I could do anything.
I was anything.

Here on the ground a caterpillar flies, the stars never change, I'll never die,
Old Willow of the blue sky!

My gray sacrifice accepted the tree passed bark to me.
Eat, the branches whispered, *drink* from my immortal cup of leaves.
How comforting to know I was saved.

Now as I walk down a road gouged by moonlight cutting ice
The field beside me heaves, can't breathe under the weight of snow
And I am too cold to waste any on heaven.
Unchanged by time the willow stands at the roadway's end
I kneel before its enveloping arms black in moonlight
and wrapping me in the promises I didn't keep
Pushing me to the sound of my returning shadow
Pushing me into the deep.

Lost Children

An old man stood in the hallway
where the photographs of my children
smiled into his heavy eyes

"I lived here once."
Light from a time of oil lamps and iron sinks
pooled yellow around his feet.
"I had a boy and girl too—are those yours—
Maybe you found a slingshot
I know it's here—someplace."

The old man's hand drifted in the air,
he mumbled to himself and never left.

His shoe fits me well.

I walk with him to where light weaves its veil
between worlds but the passage through finds vapor,
one dimensional spirits summoned by memory
while I want children who run, laugh, play forever
with their doll, bat, truck—slingshot.
No babies here.
No tears to kiss.
What was is forever out of reach.

Down the hallway of my house
his voice blows cold.
In the reflection on photographs
behind impenetrable barriers of glass
I see myself
An old man
Mumbling about lost toys.

I'm Back

Dick

    Jane

       Good old Spot

        Don't you know me?

Football

I'd like to play QB for the Cleveland Browns
or at least wide receiver

Instead

I throw a stick to my dog running a skinny post
who in the middle of the play stops to pee,
sprint my route through the kitchen when she signals
"out" by pawing the bells on the door.

Back inside she immediately rings them again.

Eyes closed I hear the crowd roar.

An Old Man's Will

Her face would have fit in nicely with the sepia and pale white of a
    daguerreotype
except she had decided on a more modern look—over painting her face,
eyes and hair too brightly colored for an old woman, especially one who
wanted her husband to die, but not too soon.

    "Sign Papa."

She had known men in occupied towns, in camps where her blonde
    hair paid
for a potato or piece of bread. This was different. A house!

    "Sign Papa."

He bought it before they married. She decorated with silver plate and
    veneer,
plastic fruit in plastic bowls, cared for him in her own way.

    "Sign Papa"

Spidery hand clutching the deed she leaned glossy red lips closer to the bed;
his uneaten dinner cold on the table she served him a pen.

        old man   old man

Withered fingers, deep tobacco stained
thin flesh, knobby bones, mumbling...

...about a girl he once loved on a bed of sunlit grass...

    "Yes, Papa, good. Now sign."

He looked at her confused.
With shaking hand he took the paper and pen.
The old woman smiled.
He did too then kissed the air before saying,

"No."

A Talk in the By and By

Damn that old woman, always going about, making a racket,
a man can't get a bit of peace around here.
Never heard her this loud before.
Sorry, son, but you know your mother,
might as well talk to that wall.

Hunted the low country today—you'll be with me tomorrow—
mud thick as pig shit, sank my boots halfway up the laces,
got a few squirrels but that ain't a buck.
Need you tracking. Tomorrow you'll bring us luck.

It's cold and wet, streams clear, no ice, and if we don't hunt we'll fish
like we've always done this time of year,
maybe poke about, our shadows crossing the hill,
yep, tomorrow, they again will.

What's that? You trying to say something?
Can't hear a thing with her out there banging away on those pots and pans.
Maybe you're asking why all the cleaning. Hell if I know.
Let me help you sit up, nothing wrong with you two men
and a little straightening can't fix.

Nothing...

Want that little wood donkey I whittled for you? I think you was five.
Might be in the barn. You gave it a name. Don't remember what. Do you?
Better if you just keep doing what you're doing,
sleep 'till tomorrow. I'll sit here, hold your hand,
make sure she doesn't barge in wanting to rattle and scrub.

Damn old woman.
Damn all that noise.

Together Alone

Listen to the wind.
Is that your heart or my own?
Cleb Johnson knows.
Here he lies:
Kicked by a mule
Dead 25
"Truth is, we're all buried,
I'm just below ground."
Twilight of a ruptured sky,
beautiful, isn't it?
Or is it raining?
Want some wine?
Is your hand cold or is it mine?

Unfinished Work

A hand lettered sign over an empty vegetable stand
Native Corn For Sale, no price.
"Got anything to drink?" I ask.
The little girl smiles. Her mother looks at me.
Behind them a large barn, new walls on one side, casts its shadow.
A man fell, died roofing it in summer.
"Think it'll ever get done?"
The little girl takes her mother's hand.

It's winter cold today, unusual for August,
the rocking chair, pipe-in-hand time after a day's work
when pie's cooling in the window
and rising pipe smoke curls toward honey colored clouds—
reminds me, have to check on the bees.
A good woman in the kitchen.
My little daughter.
Got to get up early but it's Thursday so we'll make time
and turn on the radio for The Anderson Family.
The corn's ready for picking.
Heel's loose, need to fix it, no money for a new boot.

The girl hands me a bucket of nails.
I stack a board against the barn and climb its roof.
Cold today, but I know it's summer.
I smell mother's apple pie.

Skin Deep

Tight floral shorts on a Hampton Beach woman
pushed her body mass up to a dangerously unstable position.
A slip? A trip? The sun too bright for her to see a driftwood in the sand?
Only the man's needle thin arms jabbing into her chest prevented her
from crashing down onto his white belly veined with black hair.

Why waste fate.
Wanting feeling, they entwined legs and settled for exposure.

Between Madam Marie's Mystic Parlor and a shed where roaches
swam in the used cooking oil from Irene's Grill & Funnel Cake stand,
blue neon *Tattoos* welcomed them in.

They chose the same,
Love with a heart.

Coach

Of course he never played.
That's a requirement
for those who lean their armpits into faces,
yell at players and refs,
(*do you believe this shit?*)
spill beer on children watching the game
with big eyes.

OK, he's an oaf.
What about pressed-in Tim?

A cubicle for a job,
A cubicle for a wife.
First rule for a poser: learn the jargon.
It's called a pitch and I'm your coach!
Second rule, demand respect
even from a dandelion picking (on the pitch, no less)
soccer team of little boys.

Go to the net, goddammit!
frustration at imperfection understandable,
his dexterity proven everyday in the skillful way
he moves a mouse under a sickly green computer screen.

The boys listen.
Especially his son.

Reception Room

Because of their brightness exuberant colors fade and die,
gray-white, never young, is eternal. Add vinyl, a square shape,
stubby wooden legs its only style and the chair would be perfect
for cockroaches eating strontium 90 to picnic on in a post-apocalyptic
        world.

The dentist's reception room has four such chairs and a gray-white sofa
without pillows. Almost invisible stick lamps. Magazines about pets
and dental implants. The walls are ashen.

Without color, without a real face, the receptionist sits unmoving
behind a typewriter, no computer for her, but she does have The Book
that measures out lives in 6 month appointments, each one
ending with a final no-show.

Blandness isn't reassuring when awaiting the inevitable.

The receptionist crosses out a name.

"Next."

Perspective

I saw a boy, his baseball cap on backwards,
eyes missing behind silver reflective sunglasses.
His play to break, he pulled the bough down.

Eyeless boy too old to swing on branches,
too young to hear the snapping wood cry.

News Flash

I don't understand

A comedian died, a nice man the panel of reporters agreed,
35 years ago he starred in a popular sit-com
I never saw any episodes but I'm sorry he's dead
But why did The News spend twenty minutes on him
and only five reporting a fire that killed nine children?
Under his pleasant face a news ticker shot past:
a boulder fell on a boat of tourists, all drowned.
"I grew up with him. My whole family watched his show.
I can't believe he's gone," sincere glistening in the reporter's eyes.
God has important cosmic business to handle,
She can't be responsible for making sure a few children
don't suffocate in water or smoke
But a news programmer? They're human.

...BREAKING NEWS ....Disinterested viewers...First season
of children's lives cancelled...

I don't understand

Silent Sound

Silence is not a table of wood
lacquer swirls with the heartbeat
of insects secreting resin
Stone resting against stone
pound a low-voiced drum
while parched fissured clay
snaps apart like a broken violin string

In a snow storm of rust
Iron shudders from the cold
Lost bottles cry hearing
tick tock drops of rain
measure passing time.

The bell tolls silently
its clapper thudding into
compacted useless words
But in the fullness of the space
between bronze tongue and lip
the bell's one note sings out

Silence isn't a wooden table
It's noise best left unsaid

Empty Thoughts

On a black hill
in moonless
starless night
she stands alone

A wind of myrrh
braids her hair
the stars
the moon
add rings of light
to the long ebony strands
flowing into midnight

How gentle her eyes
how tender to my lips
in the rising dawn
of spectral mists.

My mind cries.
I understand
It feels, sees,
paints words

But my heart is mute

No stars
No moon
No scented wind
or ghostly kiss

I stand alone
watching her wait
inside silence

If only I could speak

Jennifer's Room

The thrashing bold rumble of thunder madness ended,
in the afterglow from the storm's fury branches tap gently
on Jennifer's bedroom window.

Orchid people made of tissue play across old cracked walls
with blue zebras and giraffes wearing monocles.
Calico ears drooping, a dog spins his top hat of silver foil
while prancing over cardboard grass.

Jennifer's mom is an artist who works in a bar.
Rain leaks into the house but never here,
the room protected by a circle of paper and paste.

On a salvaged table decorated with rainbows
a big moon clock moves its hands toward midnight.
Jennifer is asleep in my arms. Her mother works late.
I wonder...

Would she make a little lion for me?

Jennifer is afraid of thunder but so am I.
Gently I brush a dark ringlet from her eye.

Relationship

Popcorn Beer and Candy
Look! A bunch of helium moons
Candy apple red Lizard Man green balloons
Where the smiles of clowns dangle
Like a mobile of white taffy

I see you're not happy.

This path turns into shadow filled woods
Don't stop let's keep going
I'm not afraid of that monster's moaning
Or maybe it's a wolf with hunger pains
Who sees that you're small
And easy to maim

A snake ! Ha! Got ya!
It's just an old stick!
What a great scare
What a clever trick
To cause a fright so big
With only a slimy black twig

Don't be mad
There's other ways
I can play all day
OK I know we have bills to pay

But I want to write poems and stories
Not get a job, that would be boring
Unless as a professor of English Lit
I can meet publishers who'll admire
my talent and wit

You want something else?
Sure, I'll hold your hand
Right after I follow these
Tracks in the sand
Destiny is a few steps away
Call it fate

Call it a hunch—

I'm hungry
Hope you brought lunch

Illusive Reality

Trees

thin black lines
visible under a translucent coating of ice crackle glaze
shimmer in front of snow stretched by the wind
over a glacial cascade of rocks
a white canvas for this pen and ink drawing
where the weeping birch grow

   There is no pen or ink.

Wind swirls

scrape with crystal needles
figure 8s across pools of frozen moonlight
lit by electrified ice floating through mist

   There are no numbers.

Sifting down, Sunlight inside spring water
burnishes fish scales bright acidic yellow
as the stream's golden flow coats in amber
the frogs and stoneflies in the muskgrass
of its sunglow bank

   Colors are perception,
   optical illusions existing only in the mind.

Nature

is without beauty.
Tornados, earthquakes, fire and ice,
it breathes destruction and the raw death of its poison is in us.
Except for a subjective reality
more powerful than pirouetting ice cycles
or the crying trees we think we see
we would all be cannibals

Love.

We have a mind but more importantly a heart.

Journey's End

Broad whale bone of highway of the bone white blinding
built from beached animals fed red tide, shrieks with the sound
of black semis carrying barrels of rotted fish and open canisters
spilling deception, the stink the lies.

Don't believe it.

Wrap aluminum foil around your head, let alien signals navigate you home,
you too can drive on this roadway of uncontrolled speed warped by the
    tracks
of others who just like you know the truth.

Be careful, listen for the blast of diesel warning tiny cars like yours to go
    faster,
change direction, blend into the fumes of secret knowledge illuminated
by the highway's pulsating lights.

If we stay on course, obey highway rules unless ordered not to,
we will be safe. There is no black and white. Only white.

Anointed with bronze and blush God's chosen one rides in each truck.
Our way is clear.
The spaceship is waiting.

.

Made in the USA
Middletown, DE
03 July 2022